marie claire

seafood

acknowledgements

Firstly, I would like to express my deepest thanks to Anne Wilson and Catie Ziller for the opportunity to write three more books and for having the clear publishing vision that I have been privileged to be a part of for the past four years. To Susan Gray, my patient and careful editor, for picking up all the 'oopses'. To Marylouise Brammer, the talented designer who has given time, love and dedication to making these books truly beautiful. To Ben Dearnley, the photographer, and Kristen Anderson, the food stylist, for blessing me with their professionalism, friendship but most of all talent for a very special six weeks— thank you for your generosity. To Anna Waddington, project manager and walking angel, for organising me and my manicness. To Jane Lawson, the new torchbearer, for listening, laughing and yumming with me. To David, Bec, Kate, Lulu and Melita for sharing my passion for food and for making work a special place. To Valli Little and Angela Tregonning for testing and tasting my recipes with me and sharing their knowledge. To Donna Hay, lady princess, gifted fellow-foodie and friend, just for being who she is. To Mum, Matt, Relle, Rhearn, Nathan, Trace, Scottie, Paulie and Kim for their positive feedback, love and patience. To Penel, Michael, Shem and Gabe for a bond and sealant in the form of love that keeps me afloat. To Jude, for doing the yards with me with such honesty and caring. To Dundee for the pearls of wisdom. To Mel, Chaska, Rod, Pete, Fish, Olivia, Annie, Daz, Col, Richie, Melanie, Sean, Anne, George, Yvette, Woody, Ulla, Glenn, Boyd, Sal, Birdie and Dave for enjoying eating as much as I enjoy cooking. Thanks too to Con at Demcos for providing the stunningly delicious seafood for this book. A huge hug and truckloads of thanks to Dun, Richie and Col for allowing us to invade their home for two weeks of shooting.

Finally, I would like to dedicate this book to my baby sister Paulie, who loves to fish with me in blind faith that one day we shall be blessed with a catch worthy of eating.

The publisher wishes to thank the following for their generosity in supplying props for the book: Accoutrement; Bison Homewares; Boda Nova; The Bay Tree; Country Road Homewear; David Jones; Domestic Pots— pieces by Lex Dickson, Phil Elson, Simon Reece, Victor Greenaway, Helen Stephens; Culti; Empire Homeware; Ikea; Papaya Studio; Wild Rhino.

Front cover: lobster kiev, page 66.

marie claire

seafood

jody vassallo

MURDOCH BOOKS®

Sydney • London • Vancouver • New York

contents

Enhance fresh seafood with marinades and bastes inspired by cuisines from around the world.

sesame oil, lemon juice, kecap manis, ginger, toasted sesame seeds—use for fish, prawns, octopus, mussel or oysters

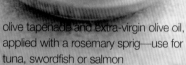

olive tapenade and extra-virgin olive oil, applied with a rosemary sprig—use for tuna, swordfish or salmon

tandoori paste, thick natural yoghurt and chopped fresh mint—use for prawns, fish, scallops or scampi

crushed mixed peppercorns, shredded preserved lemon, garlic and olive oil—use for fish, prawns, lobster or bugs

green peppercorns, hazelnut oil, orange zest and juice with fennel brush—use for squid, prawns, fish, scallops

wholegrain mustard, balsamic vinegar, honey, chives and macadamia oil—use for squid, prawns, mussels, fish, scallops

bottled chilli paste, basil leaves, shaved palm sugar and sesame oil—use for scallops, prawns, octopus, squid, fish

bottled asian sate sauce, coconut cream, lime juice and coriander— use for scallops, fish, prawns

Thread seafood onto natural skewers for extra flavour when barbecued. Try …

peeled green (raw) prawns and kaffir lime leaves on sticks of lemongrass

strips of fresh tuna woven with lemon slices onto baby branches of bay leaf

cleaned baby squid threaded onto sticks of fresh fennel

succulent scallops spiked onto slim young bamboo stalks

cubes of succulent fresh salmon
spiked onto fresh kaffir lime branches

firm white fish fillets between halved red
chillies, pierced onto thai basil sprigs

a prawn, a bay leaf and your favourite fish
skewered onto thin sticks of sugar cane

blocks of swordfish and slices of lemon
pierced with a sprig of fragrant rosemary

Salmon roe—those bright orange
bubbles that burst in your mouth—
are the eggs of the female fish.

bruschetta with salmon tartare and roe bubbles

1 woodfired italian loaf, cut into
1 cm (1/2 inch) thick slices
3 peeled cloves garlic, cut in half
extra-virgin olive oil
500 g (1 lb) skinless salmon fillets
2 tablespoons snipped fresh chives
2 tablespoons lime juice
2 tablespoons extra-virgin olive oil,
extra
salt and cracked black pepper
100 g (31/2 oz) crème fraîche
50 g (13/4 oz) salmon roe

Toast both sides of the bread until
golden, then rub one side of each slice
with the halved garlic cloves and brush
generously with olive oil.
Cut the salmon fillets into a 1 cm
(1/2 inch) dice, place in a non-metallic
bowl with the chives, lime juice and
olive oil and season with salt and
cracked black pepper.
Serve this salmon tartare immediately
on the slices of bruschetta, topped
with a small spoonful each of crème
fraîche and salmon roe.

Serves 6

Dashi granules, made from dried tuna flakes and seaweed, are used in Japanese cooking to make stock.

prawns in blankets with a tokyo dipping sauce

Cut the wonton wrappers in half on the diagonal. Take one of these triangles and wrap half of it around the centre of a prawn. Brush the end with water and press firmly to seal. Wrap the remaining prawns in the same manner.
Heat the oil in a wok to 180°C (350°F), or until a cube of bread browns in 15 seconds when added to the oil. Cook the prawns in batches for 2–3 minutes or until crisp, golden and cooked through.
To make the dipping sauce, place the dashi granules, water, shoyu and mirin in a bowl and whisk to combine. Serve prawns immediately with the dipping sauce.

Serves 4

270 g (9 oz) packet wonton wrappers
1 kg (2 lb) green (raw) prawns (shrimp), peeled and deveined, tails left intact
oil, for deep-frying

Tokyo dipping sauce
1/4 teaspoon dashi granules
1/2 cup hot water
2 tablespoons shoyu (japanese soy sauce)
2 tablespoons mirin (sweet rice wine)

Verjuice is a sour liquid made from unripe grapes. If unavailable, use white wine vinegar instead.

scallops with warm butter and shallot dressing

16 scallops on their shells
3 french shallots, finely chopped
120 ml (4 fl oz) verjuice
100 g (3½ oz) butter, chilled and cut into 1 cm (½ inch) cubes
1 roma tomato, finely chopped
2 spring (green) onions, green part only, thinly sliced
salt and pepper
2 tablespoons extra-virgin olive oil

Remove the roe and black muscle from the scallops, then remove the scallops from their shells. Rinse and dry the shells and set aside for serving. Place the shallots and verjuice in a small saucepan and bring to the boil. Cook for 2 minutes or until reduced by a third. Remove from the heat and whisk in the butter, a cube at a time. Stir through the tomato and spring onions and season generously with salt and pepper. Set aside. Heat the olive oil in a frying pan and cook the scallops in batches over a high heat for 1 minute on each side. Return the scallops to their shells and drizzle over the warm butter dressing.

Serves 4

Scampi, or Dublin Bay prawns, look similar to prawns but have thicker shells and longer claws.

barbecued scampi bathed in honey vinaigrette

Heat a lightly oiled barbecue plate until hot and cook the scampi over a high heat until they are pink and tender. Place the garlic, mustard, honey, vinegar, lime juice and olive oil in a saucepan, add the butter and heat until boiling. Stir through the dill and pour the dressing over the scampi. Serve immediately with crusty bread.

Serves 4–6

20 scampi, heads removed and
    tails cut in half
3 cloves garlic, crushed
2 tablespoons wholegrain mustard
3 tablespoons honey
1 tablespoon balsamic vinegar
3 tablespoons lime juice
1/2 cup light olive oil
30 g (1 oz) butter
2 tablespoons chopped fresh dill
crusty bread, to serve

chu chee prawns and scallops

Chu Chee paste
10 large dried red chillies
1 teaspoon coriander seeds
1 tablespoon white peppercorns
1 tablespoon shrimp paste
10 kaffir lime leaves, finely shredded
2 teaspoons grated kaffir lime rind
1 tablespoon chopped fresh
coriander (cilantro) stalk and root
1 stalk lemongrass, white part only,
finely chopped
3 tablespoons chopped fresh galangal
1 tablespoon chopped krachai
6 cloves garlic, chopped
10 red asian shallots, chopped

500 ml (16 fl oz) coconut cream—
do not shake the can
500 g (1 lb) green (raw) medium
king prawns (shrimp), peeled
and deveined
500 g (1 lb) queensland scallops
2–3 tablespoons fish sauce
3 tablespoons grated palm sugar
8 kaffir lime leaves, finely shredded
1 cup thai basil leaves

Preheat the oven to 180°C (350°C/
Gas 4). Soak the chillies in a small bowl
of hot water for 10 minutes. Drain,
remove the seeds and roughly chop.
Place the coriander seeds, peppercorns
and shrimp paste onto a foil-lined tray
and bake for 5 minutes or until fragrant.
Place these ingredients, plus all the
remaining chu chee paste ingredients,
into a food processor and process until
the mixture forms a smooth paste.
Add a little water if the paste is too stiff.
Spoon 1 cup of the thick coconut
cream from the top of the can into a
wok and heat until just boiling. Stir in
5 tablespoons of the chu chee paste,
reduce the heat and simmer for 10
minutes or until the oil begins to
separate. Stir in the remaining coconut
cream, prawns and scallops and cook
for 5 minutes. Add the fish sauce, palm
sugar and kaffir lime leaves and cook
for 3 minutes. Stir through half the basil
and garnish with the remaining leaves.

Serves 4

oysters three ways

Serve up this mixed platter of oysters.

To make bloody mary shots, place six oysters in six shot glasses, divide the vodka between the glasses, top with tomato juice, place a stick of celery into each one and season with tabasco, worcestershire and salt and pepper.
Makes 6

Place the soy sauce, sesame oil, mirin and sugar in a small saucepan and heat until the sugar dissolves. Cut the cucumber into fine ribbons and place in the bottom of the shell. Top with an oyster, drizzle with the sauce and sprinkle with ginger and sesame seeds.
Makes 12

Grill the prosciutto until crispy and allow to cool slightly before breaking into bite-sized shards. To make the salsa, combine the tomato, capsicums, onion, coriander leaves and balsamic vinegar in a bowl. Serve some salsa and prosciutto shards on each oyster, then top with a dollop of crème fraîche.
Makes 12

2 1/2 dozen fresh oysters

Bloody mary shot
3 tablespoons vodka
1/2 cup tomato juice
1 stalk celery, cut into small sticks
dash of tabasco sauce
dash of worcestershire sauce
salt and pepper

Cucumber, ginger and sesame
1/4 cup japanese soy sauce
1 teaspoon sesame oil
1 tablespoon mirin (sweet rice wine)
1 teaspoon sugar
1 lebanese cucumber
2 tablespoons pickled ginger
2 tablespoons toasted sesame seeds

Prosciutto and balsamic vinegar salsa
4 slices prosciutto
1 roma tomato, finely diced
1/2 red capsicum (pepper), diced
1/2 yellow capsicum (pepper), diced
1 small red onion, finely chopped
1 tablespoon chopped fresh coriander
   (cilantro) leaves
2 tablespoons balsamic vinegar
2 tablespoons crème fraîche

Used widely in Thai cooking,
garlic, pepper and coriander root
make a wonderful combination.

garlic pepper prawns with green chilli dip

2 tablespoons peanut oil
4 tablespoons chopped coriander
(cilantro) root and stem
4 cloves garlic, roughly chopped
1 tablespoon white peppercorns
2 tablespoons grated palm sugar
2 tablespoons fish sauce
24 green (raw) king prawns (shrimp)

Green chilli dip
2 tablespoons chopped coriander
(cilantro) root and stem
2 cloves garlic, finely chopped
2 green chillies, finely chopped
4 tablespoons lime juice
2 tablespoons palm sugar
2 tablespoons fish sauce

Place the oil, coriander, garlic, white peppercorns, palm sugar and fish sauce into a food processor or mortar and pestle and process or pound to form a paste. Place the prawns in a shallow, non-metallic dish, add the paste and toss to coat. Cover and refrigerate for 3 hours.
Place all the dip ingredients in a bowl and stir to dissolve the sugar.
Once the prawns have marinated, preheat a barbecue to high and cook the prawns until they are pink and tender. Serve immediately with the dipping sauce.

Serves 4

Saffron—the orange stigma of the crocus flower—is the world's most expensive spice.

mussels with saffron, lemongrass and tomatoes

Scrub the mussels and remove the hairy beards. Discard any that have opened or have broken shells. Heat the oil in a large saucepan and fry the onion, shallots and lemongrass until golden. Add the saffron and tomatoes and cook for 5 minutes or until the tomatoes start to soften. Add the wine and water and bring to the boil. Boil, covered, for 15 minutes. Add the mussels to the saucepan and cook, covered, for 5 minutes, shaking the pan occasionally until the mussels have opened. Discard any mussels that do not open. Stir through the garlic, sugar and parsley, and season with salt and cracked black pepper. Serve immediately with crusty bread.

Serves 4

1.5 kg (3 lb) black mussels
2 tablespoons olive oil
1 onion, finely chopped
6 french shallots, finely chopped
2 stalks lemongrass, white part only, finely chopped
pinch saffron threads
6 roma tomatoes, chopped
1 cup dry white wine
1/2 cup water
2 cloves garlic, crushed
2 teaspoons sugar
2 tablespoons chopped fresh flat-leaf parsley
salt and cracked black pepper
crusty bread, to serve

To clean squid, gently pull the
tentacles down to remove the
insides, then peel away the skin.

baby squid with caper flowers

1 kg (2 lb) baby squid
1 cup plain (all-purpose) flour
2 cloves garlic, crushed
pinch cayenne pepper
sea salt and pepper
oil, for deep-frying
2 tablespoons salted baby capers
1 cup chopped fresh flat-leaf parsley
lemon wedges, to serve

Clean the squid and cut the hoods into
1 cm ($1/2$ inch) thick rings. Pat dry with
absorbent paper.
Place the flour, garlic, cayenne pepper
and salt and pepper in a bowl and mix
to combine. Toss the squid in the flour
mixture in batches, shaking well to
remove any excess flour.
Heat the oil in a large saucepan until a
cube of bread browns in 15 seconds
when added to the pan. Deep-fry the
squid in batches for 2 minutes or until
crisp and golden. Sprinkle with extra
sea salt and drain on absorbent paper.
Deep-fry the capers for 30 seconds
or until they open out into flowers.
Place the capers, squid and parsley in
a bowl and toss to combine. Sprinkle
with a little more sea salt and serve
with wedges of lemon.

Serves 4

There are about 250 varieties of snapper. Red snapper is highly regarded for its firm, sweet flesh.

snapper pies

Preheat the oven to 220°C (425°F/ Gas 7). Heat the oil in a deep frying pan, add the onions and stir over a medium heat for 20 minutes or until the onion is slightly caramelised. Add the fish stock, bring to the boil and cook for 10 minutes or until the liquid is nearly evaporated. Stir in the cream and bring to the boil. Reduce the heat and simmer for 20 minutes, or until the liquid is reduced by half. Divide half the sauce among four 2-cup capacity ramekins. Place some fish pieces in each ramekin and top with the remaining sauce. Cut the pastry sheets slightly larger than the tops of the ramekins. Brush the edges of the pastry with a little of the egg, press the pastry onto the ramekins and brush the pastry top with the remaining beaten egg. Bake for 30 minutes, or until well puffed.

Serves 4

2 tablespoons olive oil
4 onions, thinly sliced
1 1/2 cups fish stock
3 1/2 cups cream
1 kg (2 lb) skinless snapper fillets, cut into large pieces
2 sheets ready-rolled puff pastry, thawed
1 egg, lightly beaten

An octopus survives on a diet of clams and scallops. These contribute to its sweet flavour.

chargrilled baby octopus

2 kg (4 lb) baby octopus
375 ml (12 fl oz) red wine
3 tablespoons balsamic vinegar
2 tablespoons soy sauce
1/2 cup sweet chilli sauce
1 cup thai basil leaves,
to serve

Clean the octopus, taking care not to break the ink sacs.
Place the octopus, red wine and balsamic vinegar in a large, non-aluminium saucepan and bring to the boil. Reduce the heat and simmer for 15 minutes or until just tender. Drain and transfer to a bowl. Add the soy sauce and sweet chilli sauce.
Heat a barbecue chargrill to high and cook the octopus until it is sticky and slightly charred. Serve on a bed of thai basil leaves.

Serves 4

seafood risotto

Scrub the mussels and remove any that have opened. Place them in a saucepan with the white wine. Cover and cook over a medium heat for 5 minutes or until the mussels open. Remove the meat from the shells and set aside. Discard any unopened mussels. Add the fish stock and saffron to the liquid that the mussels cooked in; slowly simmer.

Heat the oil and butter in a saucepan, add the onion, leek and lime zest and cook over a medium heat for 5 minutes or until golden. Add the rice and stir for 1 minute or until translucent. Gradually add the stock to the rice, a cup at a time, stirring constantly until all the liquid has been absorbed and the risotto is creamy. Stir in half the mussels, scallops, prawns and squid and cook for 5 minutes or until tender. Heat the butter in a frying pan, add the garlic and the remaining seafood in batches and cook over a high heat until golden brown. Stir the dill through the risotto. Place the risotto in bowls and top with the seafood.

Serves 4

300 g (10 oz) mussels
200 ml (6 1/2 fl oz) dry white wine
750 ml (24 fl oz) fish stock
pinch saffron threads
2 tablespoons olive oil
30 g (1 oz) butter
1 onion, finely chopped
1 leek, sliced
2 teaspoons grated lime zest
250 g (8 oz) risotto rice (carnaroli or arborio)
300 g (10 oz) scallop meat
500 g (1 lb) green prawns (shrimp), peeled and deveined
200 g (6 1/2 oz) baby squid, cleaned and cut into rings
50 g (1 3/4 oz) butter, extra
3 cloves garlic, finely chopped
1 tablespoon chopped fresh dill

Gravlax is a Swedish recipe
for curing fresh salmon.
It takes two days to prepare.

gravlax with parmesan sheets

1 whole salmon, filleted
1 bunch dill, finely chopped
100 g (3 1/2 oz) sea salt
75 g (2 1/2 oz) sugar
1 tablespoon white peppercorns,
finely crushed
200 g (6 1/2 oz) parmesan cheese,
finely grated
sour cream, to serve
cracked black pepper, to serve
chervil, to garnish

Place one salmon fillet skin-side down in a large, shallow, non-metallic dish. Combine the dill, salt, sugar and crushed peppercorns and spread this mixture over the length of the fillet. Place the second salmon fillet on top. Cover with plastic wrap and weigh down with a chopping board and some heavy cans. Refrigerate for two days, turning the salmon as a whole piece every twelve hours and pouring off any excess liquid. When marinated, cut the salmon into wafer-thin slices.

To make the parmesan sheets, preheat the oven to 180°C (350°F/Gas 4). Thinly sprinkle the parmesan in triangle shapes onto two nonstick baking trays lined with baking paper. Bake for 10 minutes or until crisp. Top with gravlax, sour cream and black pepper. Garnish with chervil.

Serves 10–12

Tuna is a member of the mackerel family. Varieties include yellowfin, albacore, bluefin and skipjack.

herb-crusted tuna steaks with puy lentils and fetta

Preheat the oven to 220°C (425°F/ Gas 7). Heat the butter, oil, lime rind and garlic in a saucepan until the butter is melted. Add the herbs and remove from heat. Place the tuna steaks on a shallow, nonstick baking tray and pour the butter mixture over them. Cut a small, deep cross in the top of each tomato, open out gently and stuff with fetta. Place the tomatoes on a separate tray to the fish and sprinkle both trays with salt and pepper. Bake the tomatoes for 20 minutes or until soft, and bake the fish for 10–15 minutes or until tender. Boil the lentils and bay leaf together in a saucepan with enough water to cover them. When tender, drain and toss through the lemon juice, extra olive oil and any pan juices from the tuna. Serve topped with tuna and tomato.

20 g (3/4 oz) butter
2 tablespoons extra-virgin olive oil
1 teaspoon grated lime rind
2 cloves garlic, crushed
3 tablespoons chopped mixed fresh herb leaves (sage, oregano, basil, parsley)
4 tuna steaks, trimmed of any blood
8 small, vine-ripened tomatoes
100 g (3 1/2 oz) marinated fetta
sea salt and cracked black pepper
200 g (6 1/2 oz) puy lentils
1 bay leaf
1 tablespoon lemon juice
1 tablespoon extra-virgin olive oil, extra

Serves 4

The French call scallops *coquilles Saint Jacques* after the patron saint of shellfish and shellfish gatherers.

summer seafood marinara

300 g (10 oz) fresh saffron angel hair pasta
1 tablespoon extra-virgin olive oil
30 g (1 oz) butter
2 cloves garlic, finely chopped
1 large onion, finely chopped
1 small red chilli, finely chopped
600 g (1·1/4 lb) can peeled tomatoes, chopped
1 cup white wine
zest of 1 lemon
1/2 tablespoon white sugar
200 g (6 1/2 oz) scallops without roe
500 g (1 lb) raw prawns (shrimp), peeled and deveined
300 g (10 oz) clams (vongole)
salt and pepper

Cook the pasta in a large saucepan of rapidly boiling water until al dente. Drain and keep warm.

Heat the oil and butter in a large frying pan, add the garlic, onion and chilli and cook over a medium heat for 5 minutes or until soft but not golden. Add the tomatoes and wine and bring to the boil. Cook for 10 minutes or until the sauce has reduced and thickened slightly. Add the lemon zest, sugar, scallops, prawns and clams and cook, covered, for 5 minutes or until the seafood is tender. Discard any shells that do not open. Season with salt and pepper. Serve the sauce on top of the pasta.

Serves 4

Coral trout is a sweet, firm-fleshed reef fish found in the warm waters of the South Pacific.

beer-battered fish with chunky chips

Sift the flour into a bowl and season generously with salt and pepper. Whisk in the beer to form a smooth batter. Heat the oil in a deep saucepan to 180°C (350°F), or until a cube of bread browns in 15 seconds when added to the oil. Cook the potatoes in batches until they are lightly golden. Drain on crumpled absorbent paper. Return the potatoes to the oil and cook until they are crisp and golden. Sprinkle with sea salt, and keep warm. Pat the fish fillets dry with absorbent paper. Coat the fish in the prepared batter and cook in batches in the hot oil for 3–5 minutes, depending on the size and thickness of the fish. To make the tartare sauce, place all the tartare ingredients in a bowl and mix to combine. Serve with the fish.

Serves 4

1 cup plain (all-purpose) flour
sea salt and pepper
250 ml (8 fl oz) chilled beer
oil, for deep-frying
1 kg (2 lb) sebago potatoes, peeled and cut into thick wedges
4 coral trout fillets or 8 flathead fillets (depending on their size)

Tartare sauce
3/4 cup whole egg mayonnaise
1/4 cup sour cream
6 gherkins, chopped
2 tablespoons capers
2 tablespoons chopped fresh parsley

Salted black beans—also known as
Chinese black beans and fermented
soy beans—are preserved in brine.

black bean crab

I4 large blue swimmer crabs
or brown crabs
1/3 cup peanut oil
4 cloves garlic, chopped
2 tablespoons grated fresh ginger
2 onions, finely chopped
170 g (51/2 oz) can salted black beans,
rinsed and drained
1/3 cup fish stock
2 tablespoons oyster sauce
2 teaspoons fish sauce
2 tablespoons soy sauce
3 tablespoons black bean sauce
1 tablespoon caster (superfine) sugar

Clean the crabs and use a cleaver
to cut each one in half or quarters
(depending on the size of the crabs).
Heat the oil in a wok until smoking,
then cook the crab in batches until
bright orange and tender, adding
more oil with each batch if needed.
Remove the crab from the wok and
drain off all but 2 tablespoons of oil.
Add the garlic, ginger and onions to
the wok and cook over a medium
heat until golden. Stir in the black
beans, fish stock, oyster sauce, fish
sauce, soy sauce, black bean sauce
and sugar and bring to the boil.
Return the crab to the pan and
simmer for 5–10 minutes or until
heated through.

Serves 4

individual caesars with sardines

To make the dressing, place the egg into a food processor, add the garlic, lemon juice, worcestershire sauce and anchovies and process to combine. With the motor running, add the oil in a thin, steady stream until the dressing is thickened slightly. Set aside.

Place the breadcrumbs, the grated parmesan and the parsley in a bowl and mix to combine. Place the beaten eggs and milk in another bowl and whisk to combine.

Dip the sardines into the egg wash, then into the crumb mixture, and place on a paper-lined baking tray. Refrigerate for 1 hour.

Heat the oil in a deep frying pan until hot, or until a cube of bread browns in 15 seconds when added to the pan. Deep-fry the pappadams until crisp, and set aside on absorbent paper. Deep-fry the sardines in batches until crisp and golden brown.

Arrange lettuce leaves on a plate, top with prosciutto, sardines, pappadams and parmesan drizzled with dressing.

Serves 4

Dressing

1 egg
2 cloves garlic
2 tablespoons lemon juice
1/2 teaspoon worcestershire sauce
3–4 anchovy fillets
125 ml (4 fl oz) extra-virgin olive oil

1 cup dry breadcrumbs
2/3 cup grated parmesan cheese
2 tablespoons chopped fresh parsley
2 eggs, lightly beaten
1/3 cup milk
16 butterflied sardines
oil, for deep-frying
12 baby pappadams
1 baby cos lettuce, leaves separated
8 prosciutto slices, grilled until crisp
50 g (13/4 oz) parmesan cheese, shaved

Octopus and squid are cephalods—which means 'headfooted'. Their tentacles sprout from their heads.

barbecued sweet chilli seafood on banana mats

500 g (1 lb) green (raw) prawns (shrimp), peeled and deveined, tails left intact
300 g (10 oz) scallop meat
500 g (1 lb) baby squid, cleaned and hoods cut in quarters
500 g (1 lb) baby octopus, cleaned
1 cup sweet chilli sauce
1 tablespoon fish sauce
2 tablespoons lime juice
3 tablespoons peanut oil
banana leaves, cut into squares, to serve
lime wedges, to serve

Place the prawns, scallops, squid and octopus in a shallow, non-metallic bowl. In a separate bowl combine the sweet chilli sauce, fish sauce, lime juice and one tablespoon of the peanut oil. Pour the mixture over the seafood and mix gently to coat. Allow to marinate for 1 hour. Drain the seafood well and reserve the marinade. Heat the remaining oil on a barbecue hotplate. Cook the seafood in batches (depending on the size of your barbecue) over a high heat for 3–5 minutes or until tender. Drizzle each batch with a little of the leftover marinade during cooking. Pile the seafood high onto the squares of banana leaf and serve with wedges of lime, if desired.

Serves 4

Black peppercorns are the berries
of the Indian peppercorn plant. The
berries are picked unripe, then dried.

rare pepper-crusted tuna with lemon hollandaise

To make the hollandaise, place the egg yolks, mustard, lemon zest and lemon juice in a food processor and, with the motor running, add the melted butter in a thin, steady stream. Chill until ready to serve. Place the peppercorns in a mortar and pestle and pound until roughly cracked. Remove any blood from the tuna fillet, then cut the fillet into thick batons approximately 5 cm wide x 2 cm thick (2 inches x 3/4 inch). Coat the tuna on all sides with the pepper. Heat the oil in a large, nonstick frying pan, cook the tuna fillets for 30 seconds on each side, then remove from the pan and allow to stand for 5 minutes. Cut the lemon in half and squeeze the juice over the tuna. Cut the tuna into 1 cm (1/2 inch) thick slices and serve with the lemon hollandaise.

Serves 4

Lemon hollandaise
2 egg yolks
2 teaspoons dijon mustard
1 teaspoon finely grated lemon zest
1–2 tablespoons lemon juice
125 g (4 oz) butter, melted

1/3 cup black peppercorns
750 g (1 1/2 lb) tuna fillet
oil, for frying
1 lemon

Swordfish take their name from the swordlike projection that extends from their upper jaw.

swordfish stacks with salsa verde

Salsa verde
1 cup finely chopped flat-leaf parsley leaves
1 tablespoon gherkins, finely chopped
2 tablespoons baby capers
1 tablespoon chopped anchovies
4 cloves garlic, finely chopped
3 tablespoons red wine vinegar
100 ml (3$1/2$ fl oz) extra-virgin olive oil

1 large eggplant (aubergine), cut into 1 cm ($1/2$ inch) thick slices
$1/4$ cup extra-virgin olive oil
4 swordfish steaks
2 tablespoons balsamic vinegar
4 vine-ripened tomatoes
200 g (6$1/2$ oz) bocconcini
$1/2$ cup whole basil leaves

Make the salsa verde by combining the parsley, gherkins, capers, anchovies and garlic in a bowl, then whisking in the red wine vinegar and olive oil. Set aside. Brush the eggplant slices with olive oil and cook under a hot grill until golden brown on both sides. Drain on absorbent paper.

Cut the swordfish steaks into three pieces on the diagonal. Heat a little more oil in a large frying pan and cook the swordfish over a high heat until golden brown and cooked through. Leave the fish in the pan and add the balsamic vinegar. Cook until sticky. Cut the tomatoes and bocconcini into thick slices. Layer the eggplant, basil, tomato, bocconcini and swordfish and drizzle over the salsa verde dressing.

Serves 4

Place live mud crabs in the freezer several hours prior to cooking them. This puts them to sleep.

chilli mud crab

Clean the crabs and remove the hairy dead-man's fingers. Use a cleaver to cut each crab into quarters, then crack the claws with the back of the cleaver. Heat the oil in a wok until hot, or until a cube of bread browns in 15 seconds when added to the pan. Fry the crab pieces in batches until they turn bright orange. Drain off half the oil and discard. Reheat the remaining oil and cook the garlic, ginger, onions and chillies over a medium heat for 3 minutes. Stir in the sauces and sugar and bring to the boil. Return the crab to the wok and cook for 10 minutes. Finally, season with the tamarind concentrate and soy sauce and garnish with coriander leaves. Serve immediately with steamed rice.

Serves 4–6

2 mud crabs
1/2 cup peanut oil
4 cloves garlic, finely chopped
1 tablespoon grated fresh ginger
2 onions, finely chopped
4 small red chillies, seeded and
   finely chopped
1/2 cup tomato sauce (ketchup)
1/2 cup bottled asian chilli sauce
2 tablespoons sugar
1 tablespoon tamarind concentrate
1 tablespoon soy sauce
fresh coriander (cilantro) leaves,
   to garnish
steamed rice, to serve

To prevent spitting of oil, make sure the fish is absolutely dry before you add it to the wok.

whole lemongrass fish with sticky chilli sauce

1 stalk lemongrass, cut in half and into 5 cm (2 inch) lengths
1 large red snapper (800 g/1 lb 10 oz), incised in three places at its thickest part
oil, for deep-frying
5 red asian shallots, sliced
4 cloves garlic, sliced
2 tablespoons vegetable oil, extra
2 bird's-eye chillies, thinly sliced
1/2 cup grated palm sugar
4 tablespoons fish sauce
4 tablespoons tamarind concentrate
4 tablespoons lime juice
fresh coriander (cilantro) leaves, to garnish

Place lemongrass pieces into the incisions in the snapper. Heat the deep-frying oil in a wok until hot, or until a cube of bread browns in 15 seconds when added to it. Deep-fry the fish until one side is crisp and golden. Turn and cook the other side. Remove and drain on absorbent paper. Add the shallots and garlic to the wok and cook until golden. Remove. Do not overcook the shallots or garlic or they will be bitter. Heat the extra vegetable oil in a saucepan, add the chillies, palm sugar, fish sauce, tamarind concentrate and lime juice and stir until the sugar dissolves. Bring to the boil and cook until the sauce is syrupy. Pour the syrup over the crisp fish and serve immediately, garnished with the coriander leaves, shallots and garlic.

Serves 4

Sea salt flakes are made by evaporating salt water using either the heat of the sun or fire.

salt and pepper squid

Pat the squid hoods dry. Place them on a chopping board with the soft insides facing up, and use a sharp knife to make a fine diamond pattern, taking care not to cut all the way through. Cut the hoods into small rectangles and place them in a bowl. Cover with milk and lemon juice and refrigerate for 15 minutes.

Place the salt, peppercorns and sugar in a mortar and pestle or spice grinder and pound or process to a fine powder. Transfer to a bowl and stir in the cornflour. Dip the squid into the egg white, then toss to coat in the salt-and-pepper flour, shaking off any excess.

Heat the oil in a large pan or wok to 180°C (350°F), or until a cube of bread browns in 15 seconds. Cook the squid in batches until crisp and lightly golden. Serve with lime wedges.

Serves 4 as an entrée

1 kg (2 lb) baby squid, cleaned and hoods cut in half
1 cup milk
2 tablespoons lemon juice
2 tablespoons sea salt
1 1/2 tablespoons white peppercorns
2 teaspoons sugar
2 cups cornflour (cornstarch)
4 egg whites, lightly beaten
oil, for deep-frying
lime wedges, to serve

Jasmine rice, or Thai fragrant rice, is a delicately scented long-grain rice. The grains stay loose when cooked.

poached blue eye with jasmine papaya salad

1/3 cup jasmine rice
3 cloves garlic
2 small red chillies, finely chopped
1/4 cup dried shrimp
2 cups finely shredded green papaya
8 cherry tomatoes, quartered
2 tablespoons lime juice
2 tablespoons fish sauce
1 tablespoon grated light palm sugar
400 ml (13 fl oz) coconut milk
1 cup fish stock
4 kaffir lime leaves, finely shredded
2 stalks lemongrass, halved lengthwise
1 tablespoon grated fresh ginger
4 blue eye fillets, cut in half through the centre

Follow the manufacturer's instructions to cook the rice. Place the garlic, chillies and dried shrimp in a mortar and pestle and pound until combined. Transfer to a non-metallic bowl and stir in the cooked rice, papaya and tomatoes.
Place the lime juice, fish sauce and palm sugar in a bowl and whisk to combine. Pour the dressing over the salad and toss to combine.
Place the coconut milk, fish stock, lime leaves, lemongrass and ginger in a large frying pan and heat until just simmering. Add the fish and cook for 5 minutes or until tender. Remove the fish and boil the coconut milk until slightly thickened. Serve two blue eye fillets stacked on top of each other with the sauce spooned over. Accompany with a mound of green papaya salad.

Serves 4

Tagine is a Moroccan-style stew simmered with vegetables and flavoured with spices.

moroccan seafood tagine

Preheat oven to 180°C (350°F/Gas 4). Cut the fish into large cubes. Peel and devein the prawns; leave the tails intact. Heat the oil in a large casserole dish, add the onion and spices and cook over a medium heat for 5 minutes or until the onion is soft and the spices are fragrant. Add the vegetables and 2 cups of water and cook, covered in the oven, for 40 minutes. Remove the lid, add the seafood, prunes, honey and preserved lemon and cook, uncovered, for a further 10 minutes. Place the couscous in a bowl with the butter and orange blossom water and just cover with boiling water. Allow to stand for 10 minutes, or until all the liquid has been absorbed. Serve the couscous in a ring with the tagine in the centre. Sprinkle with almonds.

Serves 4

500 g (1 lb) red mullet fillets
500 g (1 lb) green (raw) prawns (shrimp)
2 tablespoons vegetable oil
1 large onion, chopped
1 teaspoon ground ginger
pinch saffron threads
2 teaspoons ground coriander
2 teaspoons ground cumin
1/2 teaspoon chilli powder
1 teaspoon ground cinnamon
300 g (10 oz) sweet potatoes,
    cut into chunks
350 g (11 oz) potatoes, cut into chunks
2 tomatoes, chopped
2 zucchini, cut into thick slices
200 g (61/2 oz) prunes
1 tablespoon honey
1 tablespoon sliced preserved lemon
300 g (10 oz) couscous
30 g (1 oz) butter
1 teaspoon orange blossom water
2 tablespoons toasted slivered almonds

Zuppa di pesce is Italian for fish soup. Use whatever fresh seafood you have available.

zuppa di pesce

500 g (1 lb) squid
500 g (1 lb) clams
500 g (1 lb) green (raw) prawns (shrimp), peeled and deveined, tails left intact
500 g (1 lb) red mullet fillets
3 tablespoons extra-virgin olive oil
1 onion, finely chopped
1 red chilli, finely chopped
3 cloves garlic, finely chopped
1 cup dry white wine
2 bay leaves
4 large vine-ripened tomatoes, peeled, seeded and chopped
3 cups fish stock
pinch saffron threads
salt and pepper
crusty italian bread, to serve

Clean all the seafood and cut the fish fillets into bite-sized pieces.

Heat the oil in a large saucepan, add the onion, chilli and garlic and cook over a low heat for 10 minutes, or until the onion is soft and golden (do not allow the onions to brown). Add the wine and bring to the boil, cooking over a high heat until reduced by half. Reduce the heat, add the bay leaves, tomatoes and stock and simmer for 5 minutes. Add the seafood. Cover and cook for 5 minutes or until the seafood is tender. Discard any clam shells that do not open. Stir in the saffron and season with salt and pepper. Serve with bread.

Serves 4–6

Cannellini beans are creamy white beans widely used in Italian cooking. If short on time, use canned beans.

summer crab and bean salad

Soak the cannellini beans in cold water overnight. Drain, place the beans in a large saucepan, cover with water and bring to the boil. Reduce the heat and simmer for 20 minutes. Drain and allow the cooked beans to cool slightly. Cook capsicum skin-side up under a hot grill until the skin blackens and blisters. Place in a plastic bag and leave to cool, then peel away the skin. Cut into strips and add to the beans. Stir in the garlic, parsley, lemon juice, olive oil, crab meat and red onion and refrigerate for 2 hours. Season generously with salt and cracked black pepper. Serve with crusty bread.

Serves 4–6

150 g (5 oz) dried cannellini beans
1 red capsicum (pepper), cut into
   large pieces
3 cloves garlic, finely chopped
1/2 cup chopped, fresh
   flat-leaf parsley
1/2 cup lemon juice
1/4 cup extra-virgin olive oil
300 g (10 oz) fresh or canned
   crab meat
1 red onion, thinly sliced
salt and cracked black pepper
crusty bread, to serve

lobster kiev

125 g (4 oz) butter, softened
2 cloves garlic, crushed
1 teaspoon lemon zest
1 tablespoon chopped fresh chives
1 tablespoon chopped fresh chervil
1 tablespoon chopped fresh parsley
4 large green (raw) lobster tails
1 cup plain (all-purpose) flour
salt and pepper
1 egg, lightly beaten
2 cups fresh white breadcrumbs
oil, to deep-fry
steamed fresh asparagus spears, to serve

Preheat the oven to 180°C (350°F/ Gas 4). Combine the butter, garlic, zest and herbs in a bowl. Spoon this mixture onto a sheet of plastic wrap and roll into a log shape. Freeze until firm. Remove the lobster meat from the shell by using scissors to cut down both sides of the shell on the underside. Peel back the soft undershell and gently pull out the flesh in one piece. Remove the black vein. Make a deep pocket down the length of each tail, taking care not to cut all the way through. Slice up the butter and place two or three disks into each pocket. Dip the tails in flour that has been seasoned with salt and pepper, then dip them in egg and then breadcrumbs. Refrigerate for 30 minutes. Deep-fry the tails in batches in hot oil for 5 minutes or until crisp and golden. Transfer to a baking tray and bake for 5 minutes, or until cooked through. Serve sliced on top of steamed asparagus.

Serves 4

salmon burgers with tzatziki

To make the tzatziki, place the cucumber, mint, garlic and yoghurt in a bowl and mix well. Set aside.

To make the patties, first place the bread in a food processor and process into crumbs. Finely chop the salmon to resemble mince. (Do not do this in the food processor—the fish will go pasty.) Place the salmon, breadcrumbs, spring onions, lemon juice, dill, cumin and egg in a bowl. Mix well. Divide the mixture into four and shape each piece into patties. Cover and refrigerate for 1 hour. Heat half the oil in a frying pan, add the fennel and cook until golden brown and slightly caramelised. Cut the bread into four and then in half through the centre.

Toast if you prefer a crisp burger. Heat the remaining oil in a nonstick frying pan and cook the patties over a medium heat for 3–5 minutes on each side. To serve, place a few leaves of your choice onto the bread base and top the burger with tzatziki, fried fennel and tomatoes.

Serves 4

Tzatziki
1 lebanese cucumber, finely chopped
2 tablespoons chopped fresh mint
2 cloves garlic, crushed
100 g (3 1/2 oz) greek-style yoghurt

2 slices white bread, crusts removed
800 g (1 lb 10 oz) salmon fillets,
    skin and bones removed
2 spring (green) onions, finely chopped
1 tablespoon lemon juice
2 tablespoons chopped fresh dill
2 teaspoons ground cumin
1 egg, lightly beaten
4 tablespoons extra-virgin olive oil
3 baby fennels, sliced
1 turkish pide bread
salad leaves, to serve
100 g (3 1/2 oz) semi-dried tomatoes,
    to serve

Throughout the Mediterranean it is possible to find a variety of pickled or preserved seafood.

mediterranean pickled seafood salad

1/4 cup olive oil
1/2 cup white wine vinegar
2/3 cup dry white wine
3 cloves garlic, thinly sliced
500 g (1 lb) black mussels, cleaned and debearded
1 kg (2 lb) baby octopus, cleaned
1 kg (2 lb) squid, cleaned and sliced
500 g (1 lb) green (raw) prawns (shrimp) peeled and deveined, tails left intact
zest of 1 lemon
zest of 1 orange
125 g (4 oz) sun-dried tomatoes in oil
4 spring (green) onions, sliced
1 tablespoon thyme leaves
1 tablespoon basil leaves, shredded
1/4 cup lemon juice
crusty bread, to serve
lemon wedges, to serve

Place the olive oil, vinegar, white wine and garlic in a saucepan. Bring to the boil and simmer over a low heat for 10 minutes. Add the mussels and cook for 5 minutes or until the shells open. Remove the mussels from the pan, discarding any that have not opened, and remove the meat from the shells, placing it into a large bowl. Add the octopus to the pickling liquid and cook for 40 minutes or until tender. Remove and add the squid and prawns and cook for 5 minutes. Drain and discard the liquid. Add the zests, tomatoes (with their oil), spring onions, thyme, basil and lemon juice to the seafood and mix to combine. Cover and refrigerate for 24–48 hours. Return to room temperature and serve with crusty bread and lemon wedges.

Serves 4

Known as tod man pla in Thailand, these fish patties are eaten as snacks with a sweet chilli sauce.

thai fish cakes with sweet chilli sauce

Combine the cucumber, chillies, sugar, water, rice vinegar and coriander in a bowl and mix well to dissolve the sugar. Set this dipping sauce aside. Place the fish, prawns and curry paste in a food processor and process to form a smooth, sticky paste. Transfer to a bowl and, with your hands, mix through the beans, lime leaves and basil. Shape tablespoons of the mixture into small balls, then flatten them with the palm of your hand. Cover and refrigerate for 1 hour. Heat the oil in a wok until hot, or until a cube of bread browns in 15 seconds when added to the oil. Cook the fish cakes in batches for 2 minutes or until browned and cooked through. Drain on absorbent paper and serve with the cucumber dipping sauce.

Serves 4–6

Cucumber dipping sauce
1 lebanese cucumber, seeded and finely diced
2 small red chillies, finely chopped
4 tablespoons grated palm sugar
1 tablespoon water
6 tablespoons rice vinegar
1 tablespoon chopped fresh coriander (cilantro) leaves

500 g (1 lb) skinless redfish fillets
200 g (6 1/2 oz) green (raw) prawns (shrimp), peeled and deveined
3 tablespoons thai red curry paste
50 g (1 3/4 oz) snake beans, sliced
4 kaffir lime leaves, finely shredded
6 thai basil leaves, shredded
oil, for deep-frying

Skordalia is the Greek name for a dish of puréed potatoes flavoured with garlic, olive oil and lemons.

salmon on skordalia with saffron–lime butter

Skordalia
500 g (1 lb) potatoes, peeled and diced
3 cloves garlic, finely chopped
juice of 1 lime
100 ml (3¹/2 fl oz) milk
150 ml (5 fl oz) virgin olive oil

Saffron–lime butter
100 g (3¹/2 oz) butter
pinch saffron threads
2 tablespoons lime juice

4 salmon fillets, approximately 200 g (6¹/2 oz) each
2 tablespoons oil, for frying
1 tablespoon lime zest, to garnish
chervil leaves, to garnish

To make the skordalia, cook the potatoes until soft, then drain and place into a food processor. Process the potato, garlic, lime juice, milk and olive oil until smooth and creamy.

To make the saffron–lime butter, melt the butter in a pan, add the saffron and lime juice and cook until the butter turns a nutty brown colour.

Pat the salmon fillets dry. Heat the oil in a frying pan and cook the salmon, skin-side down, over a high heat for 2–3 minutes on each side, or until the skin is crisp and golden brown. Turn and cook the other side.

Serve the salmon on top of the skordalia with the saffron–lime butter spooned over the top. Garnish with lime zest and chervil leaves.

Serves 4

teriyaki barbecued salmon

To make the broth, pour the liquid in which the mushrooms were soaked into a saucepan. Add the dashi granules, soy sauce, mirin and caster sugar and bring to the boil. Simmer for 5 minutes.

Place the salmon, mushrooms, teriyake marinade, honey and sesame oil into a non-metallic dish and allow to marinate for 15 minutes.

Bring a large saucepan of water to the boil and cook the noodles for 3–4 minutes or until tender. Drain.

Heat the oil on a preheated barbecue. Take the salmon and mushrooms out of the marinade and cook over a high heat for 3 minutes on each side. (Do not overcook the salmon—it should be slightly rare in the centre.) Pour the reserved marinade from the fish over during cooking.

To serve, divide the noodles among four serving bowls, pour over the broth from the mushrooms, then top with the salmon and mushrooms and sprinkle with the spring onions.

Serves 4

12 dried chinese mushrooms, rehydrated in 2 cups of boiling water
1 teaspoon dashi granules
1/4 cup japanese soy sauce
2 tablespoons mirin (sweet rice wine)
1/2 teaspoon caster (superfine) sugar
4 salmon cutlets, 150 g (5 oz) each
1/4 cup teriyaki marinade
1 tablespoon honey
1 teaspoon sesame oil
250 g (8 oz) dried soba noodles
1 tablespoon vegetable oil
2 spring (green) onions, sliced on the diagonal

Preserved vine leaves come in tins, packed in brine. If you have fresh leaves, simmer for 10 minutes.

rainbow trout smoked in vine leaves

1 cup hickory smoking chips
125 ml (4 fl oz) dry white wine
4 rainbow trout
1 lemon, thinly sliced
4 sprigs oregano
8 vine leaves

Preserved lemon butter
125 g (4 oz) butter
1 tablespoon chopped fresh oregano
1 tablespoon preserved lemon,
pith and flesh removed,
peel finely chopped
1 clove garlic, crushed

Preheat a covered barbecue until the beads turn white. Place the smoking chips and wine in a non-metallic bowl and allow to stand for 15 minutes. Pat the trout dry using absorbent paper and place a few slices of lemon and a sprig of oregano into the cavity of each fish. Wrap two vine leaves around each trout and secure with kitchen string. Scatter the smoking chips over the hot coals. Place the trout on a lightly oiled barbecue rack, cover and allow to smoke for 10 minutes or until tender. To make the preserved lemon butter, mix together the butter, oregano, lemon peel and garlic. Spread the butter on a lightly greased baking tray to a 1–2 cm ($1/2$–$3/4$ inch) thickness and freeze until solid. Cut the butter into slices and serve on top of the hot smoked trout.

Serves 4

This edition published in 2000 by Merehurst Limited,
Ferry House, 51–57 Lacy Road, Putney, London SW15 1PR.

Published by Murdoch Books®, GPO Box 1203, Sydney, NSW Australia 1045.

Photographer: Ben Dearnley
Stylist: Kristen Anderson
Concept & Design: Marylouise Brammer
Project Manager: Anna Waddington
Editor: Susan Gray
Recipe Testing: Valli Little, Angela Tregonning

CEO & Publisher: Anne Wilson
Associate Publisher: Catie Ziller
General Manager: Mark Smith
Production Manager: Liz Fitzgerald
International Sales Director: Kevin Lagden
Sales & Marketing Manager: Kathryn Harvey

A catalogue record for this book is available from the British Library.
ISBN 1 85391 916 0.

Printed by Toppan Printing Hong Kong Co. Ltd. PRINTED IN CHINA. First printed 2000.
Distributed in the UK by Macmillan, Houndmills, Basingstoke, Hampshire RG21 6XS.
Telephone (0) 1256 329242